· Eight Concert Duets ·

1

Allegro Con Moto

J. BEACH CRAGUN

Copyright MCMXXVI by Rubank, Inc., Chicago, Ill.
International Copyright Secured

2
Grazioso

5

3
Presto

9

4
Largo

5
Allegro Risoluto

13

15

6
Presto Assai

*Give proper attention to the shift of the melody from one player to the other.

7
Moderato

8
Allegro Brillante